SCHOLASTIC

Best of Dr. Jean

Puppets & Storytime

More Than 100 Delightful, Skill-Building Ideas and Activities for Early Learners

by Dr. Jean Feldman

Oral & Written Language

Imagination & Creativity

Comprehension & Sequencing

Social & Emotional Development

NEW YORK • TORONTO • LONDON • AUCKLAND • SYDNEY
MEXICO CITY • NEW DELHI • HONG KONG • BUENOS AIRES

Teaching *Resources*

To Mrs. Myers, my kindergarten and first-grade teacher

She made me feel special and she made coming to school
the most exciting thing in my life!

My wish is that the activities in this book will instill
the same love of learning in your children!

Cover illustration by Brenda Sexton
Cover and interior design by Holly Grundon
Illustration by Milk and Cookies

ISBN: 0-439-59727-7
Copyright © 2005 by Dr. Jean Feldman
Published by Scholastic Inc.
All rights reserved.
Printed in the U.S.A.

8 9 10   40   13 12 11 10 09 08

Contents

Welcome to
Best of Dr. Jean
Puppets & Storytime

Stories, poems, and puppets . . . what a magical way to nurture imaginations, develop literacy skills, and give children memories! This book is a treasure trove of tales and rhymes that children can keep in their hearts for a lifetime.

Here are just some of the skills children will develop from their experiences with stories, poems, and puppets:

- oral language
- imagination
- sequencing
- comprehension
- creative writing
- social skills
- integrating reading and writing

- self-expression
- phonological awareness
- emotional development
- identifying story elements
- awareness of genre
- extending a story

Puppets

Puppets are a charming way to capture children's attention and reinforce language skills. In these pages you'll find simple directions for making the types of puppets below from easy-to-find materials, as well as rhymes and songs children will enjoy hearing the puppets say and sing!

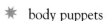

- body puppets
- finger puppets
- sock puppets
- paper puppets
- file folder puppets
- spatula puppets
- stick puppets

- paper plate puppets
- mitt puppets
- cup puppets
- spoon puppets
- paper bag puppets
- envelope puppets

Storytime

Everyone who tells a story adds to it his or her own flavor and personality. In these pages, you'll find a variety of formats that make stories come alive:

* flannel board stories
* file folder stories
* tell & draw stories
* paper cut stories
* story houses

* participation stories
* finger plays
* overhead stories
* interactive stories

Meeting the Standards

The activities in this book align with the guidelines and recommended teaching practices set out by the National Association for the Education of Young Children and the International Reading Association (1998).

Recommended teaching practices:

* share books with children and model reading behaviors
* talk about letters by name and sounds
* establish a literacy-rich environment
* reread favorite stories
* engage children in language games
* promote literacy-related play activities

Young children need developmentally appropriate experiences and teaching to support literacy learning. To this end, teachers can provide:

* positive, nurturing relationships with adults who engage in responsive conversations with individual children, model reading and writing behavior, and foster children's interest in and enjoyment of reading and writing;

* print-rich environments that provide opportunities and tools for children to see and use written language for a variety of purposes, with teachers drawing children's attention to specific letters and words;

* opportunities for children to talk about what is read and to focus on the sounds and parts of language as well as the meaning;

* teaching strategies and experiences that develop phonemic awareness, such as songs, finger plays, games, poems, and stories in which phonemic patterns such as rhyme and alliteration are salient.

Learning to Read and Write: Developmentally Appropriate Practices for Young Children
© 1998 by the National Association for the Education of Young Children.

Puppets

Set the Stage

Having a puppet theater in your room is a wonderful way to encourage children's imagination and oral language skills. You and the children can make up original productions, sing songs, or tell stories together. You can buy puppets and theaters, but children will be equally charmed by an old sock on your hand, poking through a cereal box!

Puppet Theaters

To a child's eye, once a puppet is on your hand, it's REAL! The puppet should look directly at children or at you. You can disguise your voice and let the puppet talk to children, or let the puppet whisper in your ear. You can also "translate" what the puppet says to children.

Whether it's you or the children manipulating the puppets, you can create a variety of theaters with easy-to-find materials. Here are some simple puppet theaters you can make for your room.

Cereal Box

Cut the bottom and top off a cereal or cookie box. Put any puppet on your hand and stick it up through the box. When children need to quiet down, bring down your hand to hide the puppet in the box as if the puppet is scared by noise. When they are quiet, stick the puppet back up!

Tabletop

Drape a blanket over a table. Children can crouch behind it. They can keep any props under the table.

Appliance Box

Cut off the back of a large appliance box, then cut a hole in the front. (Appliance boxes, such as refrigerator boxes or dishwasher boxes, are often available at appliance stores.) Let children decorate with paints or markers.

Door Frame

Hang a curtain or piece of fabric on a tension rod. Suspend the rod within the door frame and use for puppet performances!

The Old Lady Who Swallowed a Fly
Body Puppet

The Old Lady Who Swallowed a Fly

I know an old lady
Who swallowed a fly.
I don't know why
She swallowed a fly,
Perhaps she'll cry.

I know an old lady
Who swallowed a **spider**
That wiggled and jiggled
And tickled inside her . . .

She swallowed the **spider**
To catch the fly.
I don't know why
She swallowed a fly,
Perhaps she'll cry.

Materials: copy of page 9 (have several children color and cut out the animals in advance), crayons, two sheets poster board (one white, one colored), stockings, large self-sealing bag, construction paper, scissors, tape, markers, glue, string, stapler

How To:

1. Cut a dress from poster board (the size of your torso). Cut an apron from the white paper and glue it onto the dress.

2. Cut a six-inch circle in the center and tape the plastic bag to the back. Cut out hands and shoes from construction paper.

3. Cut the legs off the stockings and cut each leg in half. Staple the "arms" and "legs" to the body, and then staple on the hands and shoes.

4. Punch two holes at the top and string the puppet around your neck. Then sing the song and insert the animals that children have colored as you sing, facing out so children can see them in the "stomach," according to the verses (see below).

Additional verses:

Bird (How absurd she swallowed a bird)

Cat (Imagine that . . .)

Dog (What a hog . . .)

Goat (Just opened her throat and . . .)

Cow (I don't know how . . .)

Horse (This is a silly song, of course!)

Mousie
Finger Puppet

Materials: cloth garden glove, felt scraps, craft glue, two wiggle eyes, fine-tip permanent marker, scissors

How To:

1. Cut one finger off the glove as shown below.

2. Attach small felt circles for ears and nose. Glue on wiggle eyes and draw whiskers with marker.

3. Put the mouse on your finger and wiggle it as you sing this song to the tune of "The Bear Went Over the Mountain."

4. With each "squeak," make the puppet give a child a peck on the nose!

Mousie

I saw a little white mousie.

I saw a little white mousie.

I saw a little white mousie
come squeaking by my door.

So I said to the little white mousie,

I said to the little white mousie,

I said to the little white mousie,

"Come back and squeak some more."

Squeak! Squeak! Squeak!

And...

☀ Try this finger play to quiet children down:

A little mouse lived quietly in his hole.
*(Put the mouse puppet on one finger.
Wrap your other fist around the puppet.)*

When all was quiet as quiet could be . . .

Shhh! Shhh! Shhh!

Out popped he! *(Open fist and wiggle mouse.)*

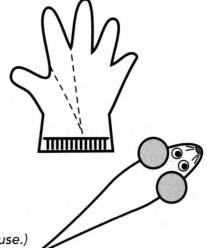

Alligator
Sock Puppet

Alligator, Alligator

See you later, alligator!

After awhile, crocodile!

Swish, swish, little fish!

Toodaloo, kangaroo!

Materials: old sock (gray, green, or brown), two large white pom-poms, two small black pom-poms, large handful of fiberfill stuffing, craft glue

How To:

1. Make a ball with the stuffing and push it all the way down into the end of the sock. This will be the head of the alligator.

2. Put your hand in the sock. Hold open your thumb and fingers to create a mouth.

3. Glue the black pom-poms to the white pom-poms to make eyes. Glue these to the head.

4. Open the alligator's mouth and have him say the chant above as he acts out each line!

And...

✳ Use the alligator puppet to focus children's attention with this chant:

A hungry old alligator's
Sneaking up on you.

And he's going to take a bite
If you don't know what to do.

So open up your ears,
And do what I say.

Are you ready? Get set!
Let's play!

Caterpillar
Sock Puppet

Materials: old sock (striped, if possible), felt, craft glue, three pom poms, pipe cleaners, scissors

How To:

1. Glue pom-poms to the toe of the sock to create a caterpillar "face." Let dry.

2. Cut a simple butterfly shape from felt. Decorate with felt scraps and pipe cleaners.

3. Turn the sock inside out and glue the butterfly to the foot of the sock. Let dry.

4. Turn the sock right side out so that it is once again a caterpillar. Place your right hand inside and wiggle your arm like a caterpillar as you begin telling the story below.

5. When the caterpillar "spins" into a chrysalis, pull the cuff of the sock over the toe. To reveal the butterfly, turn the sock inside out, insert your hand, and move the sock to resemble a butterfly in flight!

Caterpillar, Chrysalis, Butterfly!

A caterpillar crawled
to the top of a tree.
(Extend left arm. Wiggle caterpillar up left arm.)

"I think I'll take a nap," said he. So under a leaf he began to creep.

He spun a chrysalis
(Wrap left fist around caterpillar.)

And he fell asleep.
For six long months

He slept in his chrysalis bed,
'til spring came along and said,
"Wake up! Wake up!
You sleepyhead!"
(Pantomime knocking with left hand.)

Then out of the chrysalis
he did fly.
(Turn puppet inside out and move it as if flying.)

"Look! I am a butterfly!"

Elephant
Sock Puppet

Elephant Walk

Elephants walk like this and that.

They're terribly big and terribly fat.

They have no hands, they have no toes.

But, goodness gracious, what a nose!

Materials: white paper plate, sock (gray, if possible), crayons, wiggle eyes, glue, one sheet gray construction paper, scissors

How To:

1. Cut two big ears from gray construction paper.

2. Cut a circle (large enough for your forearm to fit through) from the middle of the paper plate. (You can paint or color the plate gray.)

3. Draw a mouth on the plate, glue on wiggle eyes, and glue the ears to the sides.

4. Put your hand and arm in the sock, then stick your arm through the hole to create the elephant's trunk!

5. Teach children the chant above. Let children take turns walking around like elephants.

Big-Mouth Frog
Paper Puppet

Materials: heavy green paper, scissors, markers, string or elastic, hole punch

How To:

1. Cut a frog out of green paper from the pattern on page 15. (Use a copy machine to copy the pattern onto green paper.) Fold in half.

2. Punch a hole at the top and tie on a piece of string or elastic. Hold the frog by the string and "hop" it around as you tell the story below. Open your mouth very wide, speak loudly, and exaggerate when the little frog talks (see boldface type).

And...

✳ Let children make their own frog puppets. Select five children at a time to act out this song:

> Five little speckled frogs,
> Sitting on a speckled log,
>
> Eating some most delicious
> Bugs. Yum! Yum! Yum!
>
> One jumped into the pool,
> Where it was nice and cool.
> *(One child sits.)*
>
> Now there are four little
> Speckled frogs. *(Repeat until
> there are zero.)*

Big-Mouth Frog

Once there was a little frog with a very big mouth. One day he was sitting on a log catching flies with his mother. He wondered, **"Momma frog, what do the other animals feed their babies?"**

"I don't know," she replied. "Why don't you go ask them?"

So the little frog hopped through the barnyard until he came to momma cow. **"Momma cow, what do you feed your baby calves?"**

"I feed my baby calves hay," she said. **"Oh, thank you,"** the little frog replied.

Next, he went up to momma pig. **"Momma pig, what do you feed your baby piglets?"**

"I feed my baby piglets corn," she said. **"Oh, thank you,"** the little frog replied.

Then he went down to the pond where the alligators lived. **"Momma alligator, what do you feed your baby alligators?"**

"I feed my baby alligators big-mouthed frogs!"

"Oh, I bet you don't see too many of those around here, do you?" (Say quietly with your lips pursed together to look like a small mouth.)

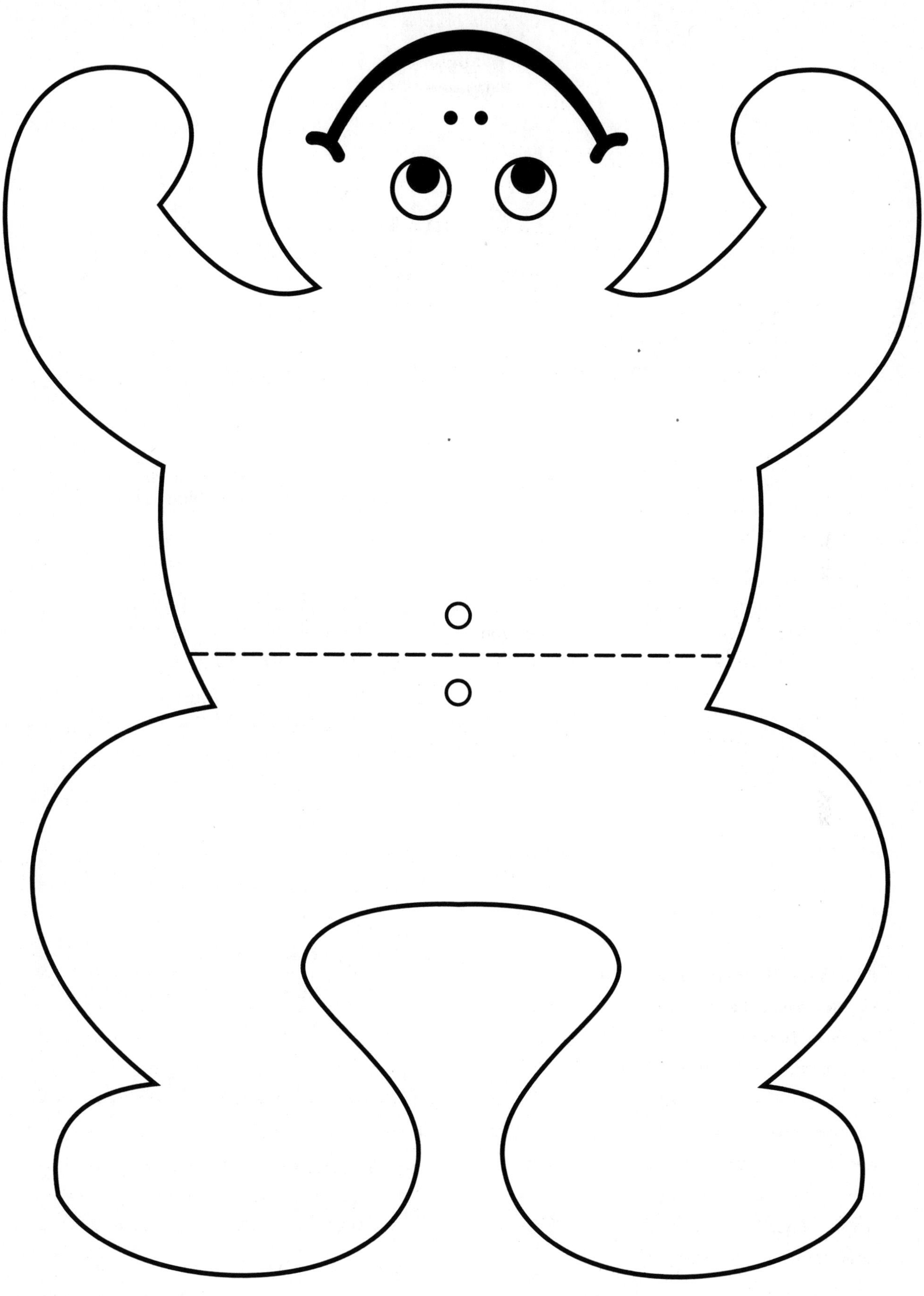

Jack & Jill
Stick Puppets

Materials: heavy paper or tagboard, markers, scissors, glue, paint stick, craft stick, wooden dowel

How To:

1. Cut out two puppets from the pattern on page 17. Color one to look like a girl (Jill). Color the other to look like a boy (Jack).

2. Glue the backs together to the stick or dowel so that when you turn the puppet back and forth, Jack is on one side and Jill is on the other.

3. Act out the nursery rhyme below with the puppet. Have children do the hand motions described.

And...

✳ Let children create their own Jack and Jill puppets.

✳ Define words like "fetch" and "crown" for children.

Jack & Jill

Jack and Jill went up the hill
(Stick thumbs up in air.)

To fetch a pail of water.
(Move thumbs up in air as if going uphill.)

Jack fell down and broke his crown,
(Bring one thumb down.)

And Jill came tumbling after.
(Bring the other thumb down in circular motion.)

Share additional verses:

Then up got Jack and said to Jill

As in his arms he took her.

"You're not hurt! Brush off that dirt.

Now, let's go and fetch that water."

So Jack and Jill went up the hill

To fetch a pail of water.

They brought it back to mother dear,

Who thanked her son and daughter.

Humpty Dumpty
Paper Puppet

Materials: heavy paper, scissors, markers

How To:

1. Copy page 19 onto heavy paper. Color and cut out.

2. Cut out holes and put your fingers through to make legs. Say the traditional Humpty Dumpty rhyme— and then a new ending!

And...

✳ Let children make their own Humpty Dumpty finger puppets. Reinforce prepositions by having them put Humpty Dumpty on their head, behind them, over their knee, beside their shoulder, and so on.

✳ Rhyme on with Humpty Dumpty! Read these verses aloud and have children fill in the last word:

Humpty Dumpty sat on a peg.
Humpty Dumpty fell on his **leg**.

Humpty Dumpty sat on a bed.
Humpty Dumpty fell on his **head**.

sat on a rose / fell on his **nose**.

sat on a pin / fell on his **chin**.

sat on a boulder / fell on his **shoulder**.

sat on a pie / fell on his **eye**.

Humpty Dumpty

Humpty Dumpty sat on a wall
Humpty Dumpty
had a great fall.
All the king's horses
and all the king's men,
couldn't put Humpty
together again.

New Ending:

So the children
got some tape and glue.
They fiddled and faddled
until he looked like new.
Then they carefully placed him
back on the wall
And they said, "Humpty
Dumpty, please don't fall!"

sat on a deer / fell on his **ear**.

sat on the land / fell on his **hand**.

sat on the sea / fell on his **knee**.

sat on a drum / fell on his **thumb**.

sat on a crack / fell on his **back**.

Humpty Dumpty said to his friend,
"I'm very tired, this is THE END!"

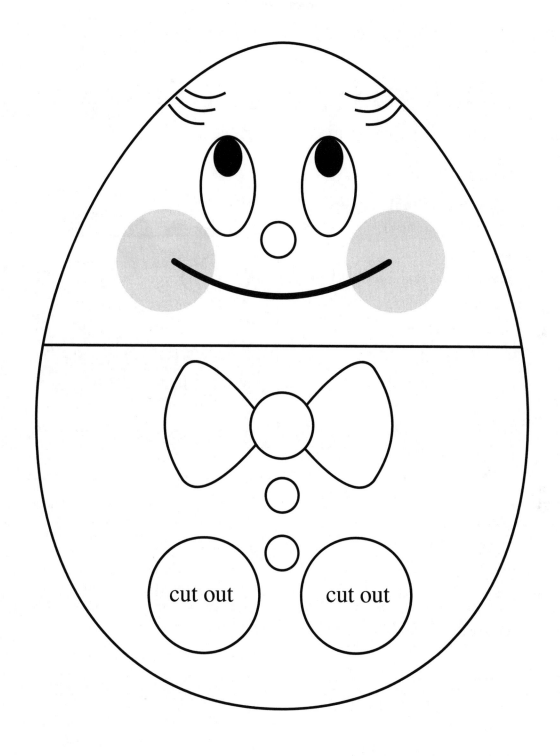

cut out

cut out

Baa, Baa, Black Sheep
File Folder Puppet

Baa, Baa, Black Sheep

Baa, baa, **black** sheep,

Have you any wool?

Yes sir, yes sir, three bags full.

One for the master,

One for the dame,

And one for the little boy

Who lives down the lane.

Baa, baa, **black** sheep,

Have you any wool?

Yes sir, yes sir, three bags full.

Materials: construction paper in black, red, yellow, green, orange, blue, and purple; file folder; markers; tape; crayons; penknife; cardboard

How To:

1. Glue a copy of page 21 to the front of a file folder. Slip a piece of cardboard into the folder, then use a penknife to cut out the gray areas indicated. Remove the cardboard.

2. Invite a child to color the rest of the page. Tape the sides of the folder together.

3. Slip the stack of colored construction paper into the file folder.

4. Remove one color at a time as you sing, "baa, baa, black sheep," or "baa, baa, red sheep," or "baa, baa, yellow sheep," and so on, depending on the color revealed.

And...

❋ For counting practice, take several paper lunch sacks and write a different numeral on each one. Set out a pile of cotton balls and invite children to put the corresponding amount into each bag.

3

2

1

Gingerbread Boy
Spatula Puppet

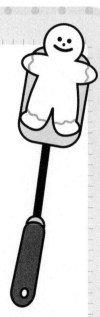

Materials: brown felt, felt or fabric scraps, rickrack, wiggle eyes, craft glue, magnetic tape, metal spatula

How To:

1. Cut a simple gingerbread boy shape from felt (see page 17; snip bottom to indicate legs). Add details with felt fabric scraps, rickrack, and wiggle eyes, and attach magnetic tape to the back.

2. Stick the gingerbread boy to the spatula as you tell the story below. Remove the gingerbread man each time he "runs," then place him back on the spatula.

The Gingerbread Man

Once there lived a man and a woman. The woman decided she would make a gingerbread boy. She got sugar and eggs and flour and, of course, ginger, and mixed it all together into dough. Then she rolled it out and carefully cut out the shape of a little boy. She put him in the oven to bake. *Mmmm!* He smelled so good. But when she opened the door to remove the pan, he jumped out and ran out the door. The man and woman chased him, but he just laughed and said:

Run, run, run, fast as you can!
You can't catch me, I'm the gingerbread man!
(*Have children join you each time you say the chant.*)

The gingerbread boy ran past some farmers working in the fields. They said, "Stop, little gingerbread boy. We want to eat you!"

The gingerbread boy only laughed as he said, "I ran away from the lady and the man, and I can run away from you, I can! I can!"

Run, run, run, fast as you can!
You can't catch me, I'm the gingerbread man!

Next, the gingerbread boy passed a cow eating grass. "Stop, little gingerbread boy," mooed the cow. "I want to eat you."

The gingerbread boy laughed even harder as he said, "I ran away from the lady and the man and the farmers, and I can run away from you, I can! I can!"

Run, run, run, fast as you can!
You can't catch me, I'm the gingerbread man!

On and on the gingerbread boy ran until he came to a river. There was a sly fox sitting near the river. "What's wrong, little boy?" the fox asked.

"Oh, dear," said the gingerbread boy. "I have to get across the river before the lady, man, farmers, and cow catch me!"

"I can help you get across the water, little boy. Get on my back."

"How do I know you won't eat me?"

"Oh, I don't even like gingerbread," the fox lied.

So the gingerbread boy hopped on the fox's back and the fox started to swim across the water. The fox said, "The water is very deep. You'd better get on my head so you don't get wet."

The gingerbread boy climbed on the fox's head. It wasn't very long before the fox said, "Little gingerbread boy, the water is deeper still. You'd better climb on my nose."

So the gingerbread boy climbed on the fox's nose and *SNIP! SNAP!* The fox opened his mouth and gobbled him up!

Tiny Tim the Turtle
Paper Plate Puppet

Materials: two paper plates, sock, permanent markers, crayons, stapler

How To:

1. Draw the face of a turtle on the sock with markers.

2. Color the outside of both plates to resemble a turtle's shell.

3. Staple the plates together along the sides.

4. Put the sock on your hand and stick it through the turtle shell.

5. Move the turtle around as you say the rhyme.

And...

✳ Use Tiny Tim to quiet children and get their attention. Explain that he is very shy, and that he'll come out only when they are quiet. When children are quiet, extend the sock and pretend to make the turtle look around at the group.

✳ Pull the turtle's head inside the shell and say:

> A little turtle lived in his shell.
>
> He liked his home very well.
>
> When he got hungry,
>
> He'd come out to eat.
> *(Stick out head.)*
>
> Then he'd go back
>
> Into his house to sleep.
> *(Pull head back into shell.)*

Tiny Tim

I had a little turtle.

His name was Tiny Tim.

I put him in the bathtub

To see if he could swim.

He drank up all the water.

He ate up all the soap.

And now he's sick in bed,

with bubbles in his throat.

B-b-b-b-b-b!
(Make bubble sounds.)

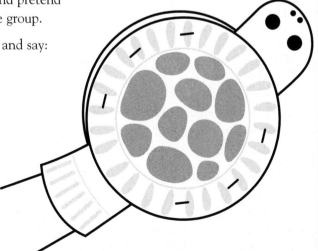

Spider
Paper Plate Puppet

The Itsy-Bitsy Spider

The itsy-bitsy spider
went up the water spout.

Down came the rain
and washed the spider out.

Out came the sun
and dried up all the rain.

And the itsy-bitsy spider
went up the spout again.

Materials: two paper plates, black construction paper cut in eight strips one inch wide, sock, permanent marker, scissors, crayons, stapler, tape

How To:

1. Draw a face on the sock for the head of the spider.

2. Decorate the two paper plates to be the front and back of the spider.

3. Bend the strips of paper back and forth, accordion style. Tape to the sides of the plate.

4. Put the sock on your hand, stick it through the spider's body, and sing the song above.

And...

✳ Have children bring old socks from home and make their own spider puppets.

✳ Use the spider puppet for acting out "Little Miss Muffet."

✳ Sing this song to the tune of "Frère Jacques." Children repeat each line after you.

> I am busy,
>
> the spider said,
>
> very, very busy,
>
> spinning my web.

Five Little Sausages
Mitt Puppet

Materials: cloth garden glove, red or brown felt, ten wiggle eyes, craft glue, Velcro, scissors

How To:

1. Cut out five simple sausage shapes (long ovals) from felt.

2. Glue on wiggle eyes.

3. Glue a piece of Velcro (hook side) to each finger on the glove.

4. Glue the fuzzy side of the Velcro to the back of each sausage.

5. Place a sausage on each finger and say the rhyme at right. Teach children to clap when you say BAM!

And...

✳ Cut sausages from construction paper and glue them to spring clothespins. Cut a circle from poster board for a pan and attach the clothespins. Remove as you say the poem (children clap on BAM!).

✳ Recite a similar poem about popcorn: *Five little kernels sizzling in a pot. The grease got hot and one went POP!* (and so on).

Five Little Sausages

Five little sausages frying in the pan.
The grease got hot and one went BAM!
(Remove a sausage, clap hands on BAM!)

Four little sausages frying in the pan.
The grease got hot and one went BAM!
(Remove a sausage, clap hands on BAM!)

Three little sausages frying in the pan.
The grease got hot and one went BAM!
(Remove a sausage, clap hands on BAM!)

Two little sausages frying in the pan.
The grease got hot and one went BAM!
(Remove a sausage, clap hands on BAM!)

One little sausage frying in the pan.
The grease got hot and it went BAM!
(Remove a sausage, clap hands on BAM!)

No little sausages frying in the pan.
The pan got hot and it went BAM!
(Clap hands on BAM!)

Five Little Monkeys
Mitt Puppet

Five Little Monkeys

Five little monkeys
swinging from a tree,

Teasing Mr. Alligator,
Can't catch me!
Can't catch me!

Along came Mr. Alligator,
quiet as can be,
And snatched a monkey
right out of that tree!
(Remove a monkey.)

Four little monkeys . . .
*(and so on, until there is
only one)*

One little monkey,
swinging from a tree.

Swung off the branch
and then he was free!

*Missed me, missed me—
Now you gotta kiss me!*

Materials: cloth garden glove (green, if possible), brown and tan felt, Velcro, wiggle eyes, craft glue, felt-tip marker, brown yarn, scissors

How To:

1. Glue a piece of Velcro (hook side) to each finger on the glove.

2. Cut five simple monkey shapes from felt. Glue Velcro (fuzzy side) and wiggle eyes to each monkey. Use pieces of yarn for arms and legs.

3. Place the monkeys on the glove, then remove them as you recite the poem above.

And...

✳ Use the puppet for another rhyme:

Five little monkeys
jumping on the bed.

One fell off
and bumped his head.

Momma called the doctor
and the doctor said,

"That's what you get for
jumping on the bed!"

Four little . . . (and so on)

Bunny
Cup Puppet

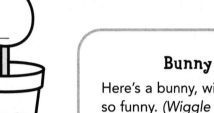

Materials: white paper, paper or foam cup, straw, pencil, markers or crayons, stapler

How To:

1. Color and cut out a simple bunny shape (small enough to fit in cup). Laminate for extra durability.

2. Staple it to the end of a straw. Poke a hole in the bottom of the cup with a pencil and push the straw through the hole.

3. Say the rhyme. Pull down on the straw so it looks like the rabbit is in a hole. Push up on the straw when the rabbit comes out of the hole!

And...

✳ Make a groundhog puppet for Groundhog Day.

Bunny

Here's a bunny, with ears so funny. *(Wiggle bunny.)*

And here's his hole in the ground. *(Pull bunny down in the cup.)*

At the slightest noise he hears, *(Have children clap softly.)*

he pricks up his ears, *(Push bunny up.)*

then hops in his hole in the ground. *(Pull bunny down again.)*

Hey Diddle Diddle
Spoon Puppet

Materials: craft glue, wooden spoon, markers, fabric scraps, yarn, wiggle eyes

How To:

1. Decorate the spoon with wiggle eyes, markers, fabric scraps, and yarn.

2. Hold up the puppet as you say the nursery rhyme.

Hey Diddle Diddle

Hey diddle, diddle, the cat and the fiddle.

The cow jumped over the moon.

The little dog laughed to see such sport,

And the dish ran away with the spoon.

Community Helpers
Paper Bag Puppets

Community Helpers

(to the tune of "Do You Know the Muffin Man?")

Do you know the firefighter,
fire fighter, firefighter?
Do you know the firefighter
who puts out flames so bright?
*(Children repeat, "Yes, we know
the firefighter . . . ")*

Repeat with:

Do you know the doctor,
doctor, doctor?

Do you know the doctor
who keeps you healthy and well?

Do you know the grocer/who sells
good food to eat?

Do you know the police officer/who
protects you day and night?

Do you know the mail carrier/who
brings the mail to you?

Materials: paper lunch bags (one per child), construction paper scraps, yarn, buttons, fabric scraps, wiggle eyes, scissors, glue, markers

How To:

1. Discuss community helpers and have children think about one they might want to be someday. Have each child decide what type of community helper puppet to make.

2. Give children paper bags and show them how to turn them upside down, put in their hands, and wiggle the bottom flaps.

3. Have children use the bottom flaps for the head and the rest for the body.

They can add arms, feet, hair, and other features with markers, or cut shapes from construction paper and glue them on.

4. Let children name their puppets and share them with classmates. Then sing the song above as each child stands up with his or her puppet when it is mentioned.

And...

* Have children bring their puppets to the dramatic play center and play "neighborhood."

* Let children make paper bag puppets of favorite book characters.

* Make paper bag puppets of animals and sing "Old MacDonald's Farm."

Puppets

Cats & Dogs
Envelope Puppets

Materials: white business envelopes, markers, paper scraps, glue, scissors

How To:

1. Cut the envelope in half as shown.

2. Decorate with markers and paper scraps to look like a cat or dog.

3. Put your fingers in the cut edge to make a hand puppet.

4. Recite an echo poem (children repeat each line after you and do hand motions described).

Cat

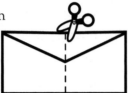

I have a cat.
(Hold fingers to face like whiskers.)

My cat is fat.
(Arms out in a circle.)

My cat wears a hat
(Put hands on head.)

My cat sees a bat.
(Clasp thumbs, "fly" hands.)

My cat sees a rat.
(Make fist and stick up pinkie finger.)

I have a cat.
(Hold fingers to face like whiskers.)

MEOW! *(Say this line together.)*

Dog

I know a little puppy.

He's thin and he is white.

And even when he's frisky

He never, ever bites.

Bow wow wow wow wow—

HOT DOG!

This Little Boy & Girl
Stick Puppets

Materials: heavy paper, crayons, scissors, tape, craft sticks

How To:

1. Have children draw a little boy or girl on paper and cut out (you can use the pattern on page 17; children can cut bottom edge to indicate legs).

2. Tape a craft stick to the back of each.

3. Have children use the puppets to act out the chant at right (substitute words as needed for boys).

And...

✳ Let children name other things the puppets should do to get ready for school. For example, "take a shower," "get their backpack," "make their bed," and so on. Let children suggest what the puppets should eat for breakfast or what they should wear.

Good Night, Good Morning

This little girl is ready for bed.
(Wiggle puppet.)

On the pillow she lays her head.
(Lay puppet down.)

Wraps the covers around her tight.
(Cover puppet with hand as a blanket.)

That's the way she spends the night.
(Rock hand.)

Morning comes, she opens her eyes.

Off with a toss the covers fly.

She jumps out of bed,
(Hold up puppet.)

Eats her breakfast,
(Pretend to feed puppet.)

And brushes her teeth.
(Pretend to brush her teeth.)

She gets dressed and
(Pretend to dress her.)

brushes her hair.
(Pretend to brush her hair.)

Now she's ready and on her way,
(Dance puppet around.)

To work and play at school all day!

People Puppets
Stick Puppets

Materials: old magazines or catalogs, photograph of each child, craft sticks or straws, tape, scissors

How To:

1. From magazines and catalogs, have children cut out people that resemble their family members. Laminate if possible. Tape to craft sticks or straws to make puppets.

2. Encourage children to use their puppets to tell classmates about their families. Or let them make up stories about their families with their puppets. Later, they can use their puppets at the dramatic play center.

3. To add to the collection, take photographs of children and cut them out. Attach to craft sticks and use them at circle time, singing the name songs below.

I Have a Friend
(to the tune of "Farmer in the Dell")

I have a friend at school.

I have a friend at school.

His/her name is _child's name_.

I have a friend at school.

Little Red Box
(to the tune of "Polly Wolly Doodle")

I wish I had a little red box

To put my _child's name_ in.

I'd take _him/her_ out and say,

"How do you do?"

And put them back again.

Hello
(to the tune of "Skip to My Lou")

Hello, _child's name_, how are you?

Hello, _child's name_, how are you?

Hello, _child's name_, how are you?

How are you this morning?

Flannel Board Storytelling

Flannel boards and felt shapes offer endless storytelling possibilities. Let the fun begin by constructing your own! Many of the stories in this section can be retold using a flannel board. Invite children to do the retelling!

Fabric Bolt

Wrap felt or flannel around a fabric bolt and use a hot-glue gun to glue in place.

Bulletin Board

Cover a section of a bulletin board with felt. Staple colorful fabric to the top and drape on the sides to make "stage curtains."

Desk

Cover the front or sides of a desk or shelf with felt (use Velcro strips to attach it without damaging the desk). Change felt colors to match holidays or seasons.

Board Game

Glue felt or flannel to an old board game. It's easy to fold up and store!

Flannel Book

Sew the left side of four or five sheets of felt together. Children can add felt pieces and make up original stories.

Little Red Hen
Flannel Board Story

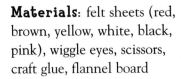

Materials: felt sheets (red, brown, yellow, white, black, pink), wiggle eyes, scissors, craft glue, flannel board

How To:

1. Cut the shapes from page 34 from felt. Add detail with felt scraps and wiggle eyes.

2. Place the pieces on the flannel board as you tell the story.

Once there was a little red hen who decided to grow some wheat. She asked the other animals in the barnyard, "Who will help me plant my wheat?"

"Not I!" said the dog.

"Not I!" said the cat.

"Not I!" said the pig.

"Well, then," said the little red hen. "I will do it all by myself." And she did.

The wheat grew tall and was ready for harvest. The little red hen said, "Who will help me pick my wheat?"

"Not I!" said the dog.

"Not I!" said the cat.

"Not I!" said the pig.

"Well, then," said the little red hen. "I will do it all by myself." And she did.

Next, the wheat had to be taken to the mill and ground into flour.

"Who will help me grind my wheat?" asked the little red hen.

"Not I!" said the dog.

"Not I!" said the cat.

"Not I!" said the pig.

"Well, then," said the little red hen. "I will do it all by myself." And she did.

Finally, the flour was ready to be made into bread. "Who will help me make my bread?" asked the little red hen.

"Not I!" said the dog.

"Not I!" said the cat.

"Not I!" said the pig.

"Well, then," said the little red hen. "I will do it all by myself." And she did.

The bread smelled so good when it was baking. All the animals' mouths were watering as they gathered around, hoping to get a piece of bread.

"Who will help me eat my bread?" asked the little red hen.

"I will!" said the dog.

"I will!" said the cat.

"I will!" said the pig.

"No!" said the little red hen. "You did not help me plant my wheat. You did not help me pick my wheat. You did not help me take it to the mill to be ground into flour. And you did not help me make my bread. I did it ALL BY MYSELF! And my little chicks and I will eat it all by ourselves!"

And they did!

(Use yarn
for tail.)

Scat the Cat
File Folder Story

Materials: file folder, crayons, markers, tape, 8- by-10-inch sheets of construction paper (two black, one blue, one red, one yellow, one green), penknife

How To:

1. Cut a simple cat shape (see above) from the front of the file folder. Insert paper in the file folder in the following order: black (to show first), blue, red, yellow, green, black.

2. Tape the sides of the file folder and invite children to decorate the front with crayons. Read the story below aloud and follow the directions. Encourage children to join in on the "chorus."

Once there was a little black cat.
(*Hold up the file folder showing the black cat.*)

He was a magic cat because he could change his colors (*snap fingers*) just like that. He just had to say:

I'm Scat the Cat. I'm sassy and fat.

And I can change my colors (snap) *just like that!*

One day Scat decided he was tired of being the same color all the time. He wanted to be a new color, so he said:

I'm Scat the Cat. I'm sassy and fat.

And I can change my colors (snap) *just like that!*

(*Remove the black paper to make the cat blue.*)

And he changed to blue! Scat went down to the pond to look at himself in the blue water, but he fell in and couldn't swim. Timmy Turtle came along and helped Scat get back on shore.

Scat decided he didn't want to be blue anymore, so he said:

I'm Scat the Cat. I'm sassy and fat.

And I can change my colors (snap) *just like that!*

(*Remove the blue paper to make the cat red.*)

And he changed to red. He went walking down the street and people started laughing at him.

Whoever heard of a red cat! they said. Scat decided he didn't want to be red anymore, so he said:

I'm Scat the Cat. I'm sassy and fat.

And I can change my colors (snap) *just like that!*

(*Remove the red paper to make the cat yellow.*)

And he changed to yellow. Scat went walking in the woods and found his cousin Leo the Lion.

Grrrrr! roared Leo. *I'm the only cat who can be yellow!*

Scat decided he'd better not be yellow anymore, so he quickly said:

I'm Scat the Cat. I'm sassy and fat.

And I can change my colors (snap) *just like that!*

(*Remove the yellow paper to make the cat green.*)

Scat wanted to play with his brothers and sisters in the grass. He tried to play with them, but he was green like the grass so they couldn't see him.

Scat decided he didn't want to be blue, or red, or yellow, or green, so he said:

I'm Scat the Cat. I'm sassy and fat.

And I can change my colors (snap) *just like that!*

(*Remove the green paper to make the cat black.*)

Scat knew that being himself was the best thing to be.

Letter Monster
File Folder Story

Materials: file folder, crayon or marker, scissors, sheet of white paper

How To:

1. Cut a large oval or circle from the front of a folder. Draw head, arms, and legs to create a monster.

2. Insert paper in the file folder and write the letters in his tummy as you recite the poem.

And...

✳ Invite children to write some of the letters in the monster's tummy as you tell the story.

Letter Monster wanted to read. He thought if he ate letters, it was all he would need!

On Monday he ate a b c.
"Mmmm, they taste so good to me!"

On Tuesday he chomped d e f g.
"Eating letters is fun as can be!"

On Wednesday he nibbled on h i j k.
"More letters, more letters, is what I say!"

On Thursday he feasted on l m n o.
"Letters are so good, you know."

On Friday he swallowed p q r s t u.
"I think letters are good for you."

On Saturday he gobbled v w x and y.
"I'm almost finished," he said with a sigh.

On Sunday he slowly ate the z.
Then he fell asleep and caught some zzzzz's!

Bingo
Tell & Draw Story

Materials:
chalkboard and chalk
(or use chart paper or
the overhead projector)

How To:
Tell children the story below
as you draw and add the
different features for all to see.

One day my dog
Bingo ran away.
I went to the park
to see if I could
find him.

When I got to the
park I accidentally
stepped in a pile
of bumblebees.
The bees swarmed
all around me.

I wanted to
get away from
the bees, so
I jumped into
a pond.

But I still needed
to find Bingo,
so I ran to the
top of a tall hill.

When I got to
the top of the
hill, I saw two
doors with little
mouseholes.

I knocked on
the doors, but
nobody was
there.

I ran down one
side of the hill.

Then I ran
down the other
side of the hill.

Has anybody
seen my dog
Bingo?

Here, Kitty, Kitty!
Tell & Draw Story

Materials: chart paper or chalkboard, marker or chalk, or use the overhead projector

How To: Tell the story below as you draw on chart paper, chalkboard, or the overhead.

Here is Timmy's house. It's made with the letter T.

It has two rooms.

Each room has a chimney and a window.

Growing outside the door is tall grass.

Here's his friend Suzie's house. It's made with the letter S.

One day Timmy went to Suzie's house to borrow some milk.

Suzie took Timmy down in the basement to get the milk.

They slipped and spilled the milk, so they went back down in the basement and got more.

Timmy took a shortcut home. He went down one valley and up a hill.

Then he went down another valley and up another hill.

He gave the milk to his special pet when he got home. Can you guess what it was?

Baby Bird
Paper Cut Story

Materials: construction paper, scissors, marker

How To:

1. Start with a sheet of paper, scissors, and marker in your lap.

2. Follow the directions as you tell the story, showing children each step.

Mother Bird decided to build a nest. (*Fold the paper in half and cut.*)

Mother Bird sat on the nest and laid a beautiful egg. (*Open the nest to reveal an egg shape.*)

Now, Mother Bird could not leave the egg. She had to sit on it and keep it warm and safe. Even when it rained and the wind blew, Mother Bird had to sit there to protect her egg.

Fortunately, two little bugs who lived in the tree made friends with Mother Bird and kept her company. This is one little bug. His name was _____. (*Use a child's name in the class. Draw a dot for the bug.*)

This is the other little bug. Her name was _____. (*Use another child's name in the class. Draw another dot on the other side.*)

One day as Mother Bird was sitting on the egg, she heard a little cracking sound. She looked down and saw a tiny little crack in her egg! (*Cut a little slit on the fold, slanted toward the eyes.*)

Then she heard a loud cracking sound. (*Cut around the eye and slit as shown, stopping before you get to the edge.*)

And guess what Mother Bird saw coming out of the big crack in her egg? She saw her baby bird! (*Open the egg and bend up the beak as shown. Put the "chick hat" like a visor on a child's head!*)

 # Pumpkin House
Paper Cut Story

Materials: orange construction paper, scissors

How To:

1. Place the orange paper and scissors in your lap.

2. As you tell the story below, cut out the different parts with the scissors as indicated.

Once there was a boy who lived in a funny orange house near _name of your school_.

His house was shaped like half a circle with the chimney at the bottom.

This boy had a cat named _child's name_. This cat had a long, curved tail, so the boy had a special door cut just for the cat's tail.

The boy always wore a funny hat. He had a special door built for himself, too, so his hat would not fall off every time he went in and out the door.

The boy also had two pet birds. Their names were _child's name_ and _child's name_. He had a window cut just for them so they could fly in and out.

It was getting close to Halloween, so all the children in _teacher's name_ class went to his house and knocked on his door. The boy came to the door and said, _Close your eyes!_

SURPRISE! It's a jack-o'-lantern!

Three Boppin' Bears
Story House

Materials: large paper bag, markers or crayons, scissors, tape, stapler, craft sticks

How To:

1. Color and cut out the three bears and Goldilocks from page 42. Tape them to craft sticks to create puppets.

2. Fold back the corners on the back of the bag and tape to make the roof of a "house."

3. Staple the bottom flap of the sack on the sides to make a pocket in which to store the puppets.

4. Turn the bag over and decorate to look like a house. Let children use the puppets to retell the story of "Goldilocks and the Three Bears," then teach them the chant below.

Once upon a time in the middle of
the woods lived the three bears.
Yeah! Yeah! Yeah!
*(Snap fingers and slap thighs in beat
with Yeah! Yeah! Yeah!)*
One was the papa bear, one was the
mama bear, and one was the wee bear.
Yeah! Yeah! Yeah!
They went to take a walk in the big
woods. Along came the girl with the
golden curls.
Her name was Goldilocks, and
upon the door she knocked,
(Pretend to knock on door.)
but no one was there. Yeah! Yeah! Yeah!
So she walked right in and had herself a
bowl of porridge. She didn't care!
(Shake head no.)
Home, home, home came the three bears.

"Someone's been eating my
porridge," said the papa bear.
Yeah! Yeah! Yeah!
"Someone's been eating my
porridge," said the mama bear.
Yeah! Yeah! Yeah!
"Ba ba ba," said the little wee bear.
"Someone's been eating my soup—
OOOH!" *(Throw arms up in the air.)*
Just then Goldie woke up—AAAH!
She broke up the party, and she beat it out
of there!
"Good-bye, good-bye, good-bye,"
said the papa bear. *(Wave.)*
"Bye, bye, bye," said the mama bear.
(Wave.)
"Ba ba ba," said the little wee bear.
(Wave.)
And so ends the story of the three bears!

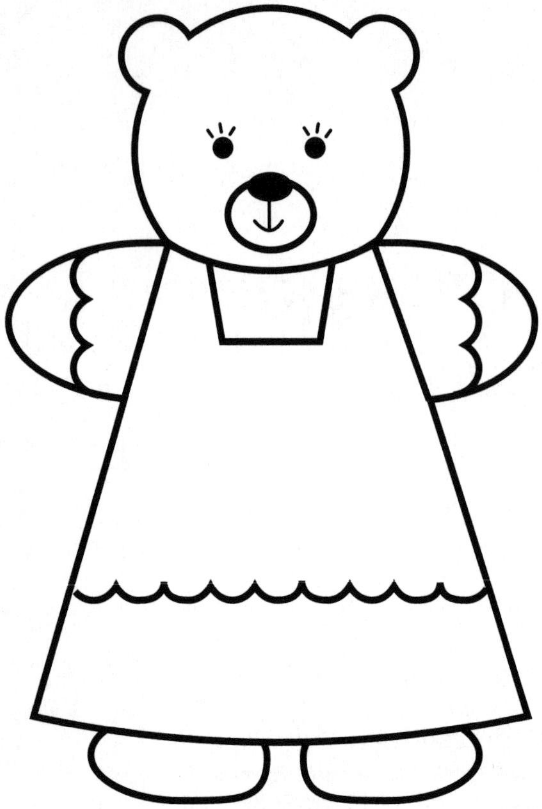

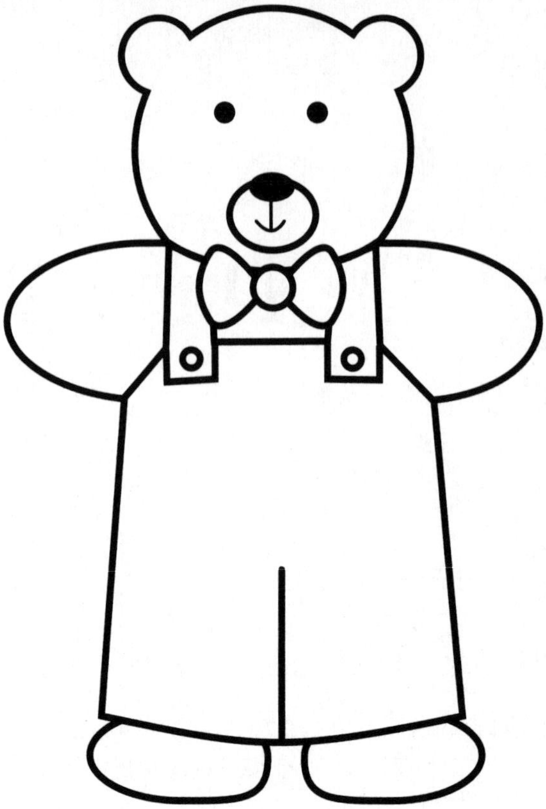

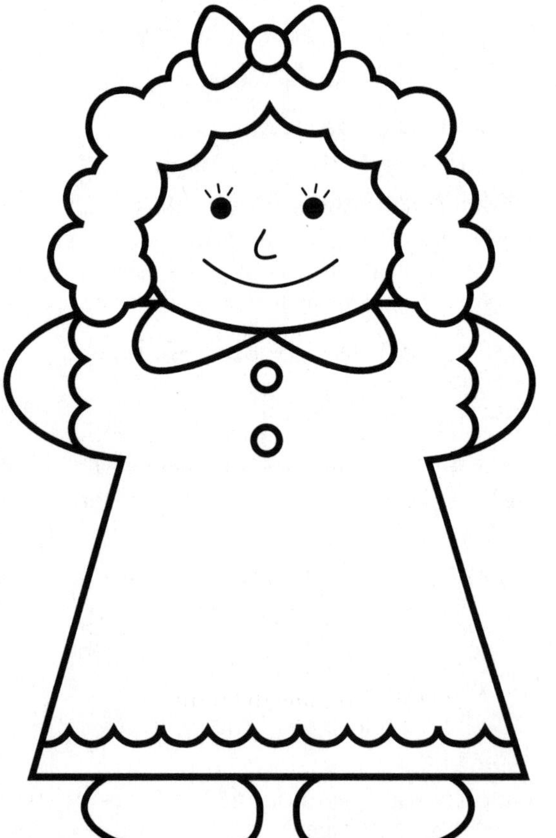

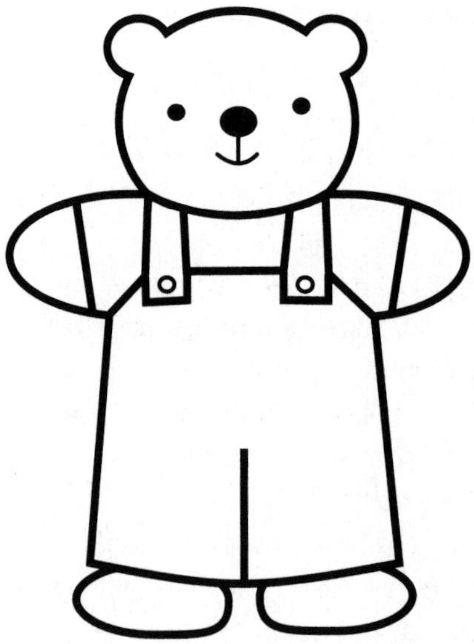

The Great, Big, Enormous Turnip
Participation Story

How To:

1. Select children to play the different characters in the story: grandpa, grandma, granddaughter, dog, cat, mouse. Have them act the story out as you read it.

2. Invite the rest of the group to join in on the chorus.

Once there was a grandpa who planted a wonderful vegetable garden. He grew corn, beans, peas, tomatoes, carrots, and many other vegetables. But his prize plant was his turnips. He grew the biggest turnips in the whole county!

One fine summer morning he decided to pull up one of those turnips for dinner. So he looked around until he found a great, big, enormous turnip. He grabbed on to the stem and . . .

CHORUS:
He pulled and pulled left.
(*Pretend to pull left.*)
He pulled and pulled right.
(*Pretend to pull right.*)
He pulled and pulled (*Pull from front.*)
With strength and might,
But he couldn't pull up the turnip.
(*Hold up palms, shrug, and shake head.*)

So grandpa went and got grandma. Grandpa pulled the turnip, grandma pulled grandpa and . . . (*Chant chorus; change beginning to "They pulled . . ."*)

So grandma went and got the dog. Grandpa pulled the turnip, grandma pulled grandpa, the dog pulled grandma and . . . (*Chant chorus.*)

So the dog went and got the cat. Grandpa pulled the turnip, grandma pulled grandpa, the dog pulled grandma, the cat pulled the dog and . . . (*Chant chorus.*)

Just then a little mouse walked by. "Whatcha doin'?" he asked.

"We're trying to pull up this great, big, enormous turnip," they all said.

"Can I help you?" asked the mouse.

"Oh, you're too small," they all replied.

"Well, let me try. I think I can help you do it," said the mouse.

So grandpa pulled the turnip, grandma pulled grandpa, the dog pulled grandma, the cat pulled the dog, the mouse pulled the cat and . . .

They pulled and pulled left.
They pulled and pulled right.
They pulled and pulled
With strength and might,
And POP! Up came the turnip.
And the little mouse said, "I told you so!"

Heidi High and Louie Low
Finger Play

Materials: marker

How To:

1. Draw little faces on your thumb.

2. Read the story below aloud. Start with your right hand in a fist.

One day Heidi High opened her door (*open four fingers on right hand*), went outside (*stick up right thumb*), and closed her door (*close fingers*). She said (*wiggle right thumb and use your high voice*), What a beautiful day! I'm going to visit my friend Louie Low. So Heidi went up the hill and down the hill and up the hill and down the hill (*move right thumb up and down in front of body until it reaches your left fist*).

She knocked on the front door and said (*pretend to knock on left fist with right hand*), Hello? Let me try the back door. (*Knock on opposite side of left fist.*) Hello? I guess he's not home. So Heidi went up the hill and down the hill and up the hill and down the hill (*move right thumb up and down back in front of your body*). When she got home, she opened her door, went inside, and shut her door (*open fingers, tuck in thumb, then close fingers to make a fist*).

The next day Louie Low opened his door (*open fingers*), went outside (*stick up left thumb*), and closed his door (*close fingers*). He said (*wiggle left thumb and use your high voice*), What a beautiful day! I'm going to go visit my friend Heidi High. (*Continue same as Heidi did on the previous day . . .*)

The next day both Heidi High and Louie Low opened their doors (*open fingers*), went outside (*stick up thumbs*), and closed their doors (*close fingers*). Heidi said (*wiggle right thumb*), What a beautiful day! I'm going to go visit my friend Louie Low. And Louie said (*wiggle left thumb*), What a beautiful day! I'm going to visit my friend Heidi High. So they both went up the hill and down the hill (*move thumbs toward each other until they meet*) until they ran into each other.

They danced and played and had the best time (*wiggle thumbs*). After a while Heidi said, Well, Louie, I better go home. And Louie said, Okay. So they gave each other a hug (*hug thumbs*), and they both went up the hill and down the hill (*wiggle thumbs apart to opposite sides of the body*). When they got home they opened their doors (*open fingers*), went inside (*tuck in thumbs*), closed their doors (*close fingers*), and went to sleep (*put hands together and lay your head on them*).

Three Little Pigs
Overhead Story

Materials: overhead projector and screen, copy of page 46, scissors, envelope

How To:

1. Cut shadow puppets from the patterns on page 46.

2. Place the figures on the overhead as you tell the story of the three little pigs. Put a different hat on each pig. Remove or rearrange the pieces as you go, according to the story.

3. Store the pieces in an envelope.

Once upon a time there were three little pigs. The first little pig built his house with straw. The second built his house with sticks. The third worked extra hard. He built his house with bricks.

One day the Big, Bad Wolf was walking by the house of the first. He was hungry, so he stopped and knocked on the door and said, "Little pig, little pig, let me come in."

The little pig replied, "Not by the hair of my chinny chin chin."

"Then I'll huff and I'll puff and I'll blow your house in," said the wolf.

So he huffed and he puffed and he blew in the first little pig's house of straw. But before the wolf could catch the first little pig, the pig ran into the house of the second little pig.

The wolf went to the house of the second little pig and knocked on the door. "Little pigs, little pigs, let me come in!"

"Not by the hair of our chinny chin chins," said the first and second little pigs.

"Then I'll huff and I'll puff, and I'll blow your house in," said the wolf. So he huffed and he puffed and he blew in the second little pig's house of sticks. But before that wolf could catch those little pigs, they ran into the house of the third little pig.

The wolf went to the house of the third little pig and knocked on the door.

"Little pigs, little pigs, let me come in," said the wolf.

"Not by the hair of our chinny chin chins," cried the three little pigs.

"Then I'll huff and I'll puff and I'll blow your house in!"

So he huffed and he puffed and he huffed and he puffed. But he could not blow down that house of bricks. Now the wolf had an idea. "I'll climb on the roof and go down the chimney." But those little pigs were very wise. They filled a big pot with water, put it in the fireplace, and started a big fire under the pot. The wolf came down the chimney. "YEOW!" He hit that pot of boiling water. He jumped so high he flew right out of that chimney.

The Big, Bad Wolf never bothered those little pigs again.

(Cut three pig shapes.)

brick house

straw house

stick house

The Star
Interactive Story

Materials: paper bag, red apple with stem intact, knife (keep away from children)

How To:

1. With the apple and knife in the bag, begin telling the story below.

2. Use names of children in your class to capture their interest!

One day _first child's name_ went to visit _his/her_ aunt. Auntie said, "How would you like to go on a secret mission?"

"Oh, I'd love that," replied _first child._

So Auntie said, "I want you to find a little red house with no doors and no windows. There should be a chimney on top and a star in the middle." _First child_ was so excited to set off on the mission. As _first child_ was thinking about what it could be, _he/she_ ran into _second child._

"Do you know where I can find a little red house with no doors and no windows? There should be a chimney on top and a star in the middle." _Second child_ said, "I've never heard of anything like that, but would you like me to help you?"

"Sure," replied _first child_ and off they went. They walked on a little farther until they saw _third child._

"Have you seen a little red house with no doors and no windows? There's a chimney on top and a star in the middle."

"Gosh. I don't know where that could be, but would you like me to help you?" replied _third child._ So off they went on their mission.

(_Continue, including as many more children as you like in the search._)

The children had almost given up when they ran into Uncle. "Uncle," the children said. "Auntie sent us on a mission. She told us to find a little red house with no doors and no windows. There's a chimney on top and a star in the middle. Where could it be?"

Uncle laughed, "Well, I have the answer to your riddle right here in my sack." And he pulled out an apple. (_Pull the apple from the sack._)

"How does that solve our riddle?" the children asked.

Uncle said, "Well, this apple is like a little red house. See, it's round and the stem is like a chimney."

"But where's the star?" wondered the children. Uncle took a knife and sliced the apple in half. (_Slice the apple in half diagonally._) There was a star in the middle!

Uncle said, "We are all like this star. We're different sizes, colors, and shapes on the outside. But if you look inside, you'll find a special star inside each person you meet!"

Eat some apples for snack!

Pumpkin Man
Interactive Story

Materials:
chart paper, marker

How To:

1. Demonstrate the movements at right and invite children to make them as you read the story.

"Knock": pretend to knock

"Rock": sway back and forth

"Spin": twirl hands around

"Come in": make hand motion

2. Draw the body parts on chart paper as shown, as you come to them in the story.

Once there was a little old lady who would sit all day and **rock** and **spin** and wait for somebody to come in. One day as she **rocked** and **spun** she heard a **knock** at the door.

"**Come in**," she called. In came two big, black boots. (*Draw boots.*) "I can't talk to big, black boots," said the little old lady.

So she sat and **rocked** and **spun** until she heard a **knock** at the door. "**Come in**," she called. And in came bony legs. (*Draw two skinny legs coming out of the boots.*) "I can't talk to two legs," said the little old lady.

So she sat and **rocked** and **spun** until she heard a **knock** at the door. "**Come in**," she called. And in came a funny body. (*Draw a pear-shaped body.*) "I can't talk to a funny body," said the little old lady.

So she sat and **rocked** and **spun** until she heard a **knock** at the door. "**Come in**," she called. And in came two wiggly arms. (*Draw wiggly arms.*) "I can't talk to wiggly arms," said the little old lady.

So she sat and **rocked** and **spun** until she heard a **knock** at the door. "**Come in**," she called. And in came two big hands. (*Draw hands at the end of the arms.*) "I can't talk to two big hands," said the little old lady.

So she sat and **rocked** and **spun** until she heard a **knock** at the door. "**Come in**," she called. And in came a big pumpkin head. (*Draw a pumpkin head on the figure.*) "Well, I *can* talk to a pumpkin man," said the little old lady. And she did!